The Wisdom of the.

CD also available from

Jackie Hagan is a comedian, performance poet, playwright and maker of *strange glittery things*. When she was six, she danced out of an oversized birthday card to the music from *War of the Worlds* as a present to her mum. She hasn't changed much. She spent her pre-teens at dance schools dressed variously as a teddy bear, a jockey, a zombie, and generally covered in hairspray and make up. Awarded "Best Emerging Poet" by The Poetry Kit and more impressively a Blue Peter badge for a bring and buy sale she never actually put on, Jackie now facilitates creative writing sessions for adults with mental health needs and performs around the UK. She makes technicoloured cakes and has multicoloured hair, enjoys teddies with one eye and people who talk weird. She does not understand scart leads or maps and hopes one day to travel around the country in a camper van drinking tea under the Moon.

You are so strong + so talented. I'm thinking of you and you are going to go far.

Jackie

Jackie Hagan

The Wisdom of the Jumble Sale

fp

Flapjack Press
www.flapjackpress.co.uk

First published in 2009 by Flapjack Press
Chiffon Way, Trinity Riverside, Gtr Manchester M3 6AB
www.flapjackpress.co.uk

Reprinted 2011

ISBN-13: 978 0 9555092 4 7

Front cover art & all internal illustrations by Brink, 2009
www.paulneads.co.uk
Back cover art: "Diazepam 3" by Jackie Hagan, 2009

Printed & bound in Great Britain by Direct-POD
Saxon Fields, Old Harborough Road, Brixworth, Northampton NN6 9BX
www.direct-pod.com

To my dad, Don Hagan
1953 – 2001
Love you

Contents

Chapter 4: The Waiting Room

Chapter 5: The Bedroom

I like people who say 'chimley' and 'crips' and get it so wrong it's a million times better than being right. I like people who smell like a pasty and can't spell their own middle name. I like it when kids gently ask what the violin's name is.

When I was little my parents let me be dead creative and weird, which was fab, and then I went to university where they believe that 2 + 2 = 4 and you're absolutely not allowed to spell it 'disslecksick'. I started to believe that the world has to run in straight lines, goal-orientated, perfectly categorised and you must always try to be normal, understood and normal. And, if possible, liked and perfect.

Like a lot of people, in my early twenties I went mad and tried to find the meaning of life. I dipped my toes in various religions, faffed about with new age wisdom, did a lot of soul searching, read loads of annoying self-help books and idolised anyone who seemed to know what they were doing. Eventually, I came to the conclusion that the wisdom I needed was all around me in the first place; in the nonsense my mum says over a cup of tea, the drunken ramblings of my friends, and the straight forward gumption of little old ladies at bus stops. It was in the attitudes of normal ordinary people around me; people who had had to cope. Common sense. Or rather, common nonsense. I realised that accepting the jumble sale quirks and chipped mugs of life, and then having a cup of tea and laughing about it, is much easier than getting to the core of existence. And that being normal, understood or liked is the icing on a cake you don't always want to eat. 'Perfect', of course, is a big pile of pretend cherries.

This book is about jumble sale wisdom and jumble sale people with bent ears and secrets in their pockets, some real, some pretend-real, and the technicoloured world we inhabit. I hope you find yourself in it.

Love and Gumption,
Jackie 𝒳

The Wisdom of the Jumble Sale

Chapter 1
The Jumble Sale

"Wisdom is biro'd on the back of everyone's hand:
Buy milk. Get leccy."

At the jumble sale no-one fails at nothing.

We laugh at nothing,
dance and drink 10p coffee.
Carebears serve Baileys
whilst Fraggles make tea
and laugh at their own shoes,
which they haven't got on.

Fat-faced dolls
wink lazy eyes,
cross chubby thighs
at teddy bears
with booze on their minds.

At the jumble sale no-one fails.
No good or bad,
just preference and dust,
endless books with chewed ears
and names in the front.

At the jumble sale
there's no death or sushi.

There's bag ladies, cat women, trampolines,
the Moon has a stall
selling Babelfish and pop-up books.

At the jumble sale religion is glitter,
badges and laughter,
and wisdom is biro'd
on the back of everyone's hand:

      Buy milk
      Get leccy

A Made-Up Town

You know the way parents don't get a handbook?
Ours didn't have any books.
They had an accent and an attitude,
so they made it up:
our imaginary town.

I was the youngest
and allowed to do whatever I liked,
but there was nowhere to go and nothing to do,
so this is my skill:

    I could make a bag of No-Frills crisps
    my best mate for the day,
    call it Barry and love it to bits,
    and then eat it and go out to play.

    I had eight imaginary friends.

Our parents didn't teach us right from wrong
in the same way
as the parents of kids I met when I left
my imaginary town.

They didn't teach us
how many continents there are,

or what continents are,

or what the point of knowing that is.

They didn't teach us about politics
but we felt its effects.

So when I left
it was hard to impress

the *other kids*.

The kids who grew up into adults who think it's clever
to laugh at people's spelling mistakes

and feel sorry for us cos we've never eaten
some sort of shit food we don't care about.
Adults who *can't believe!* we don't know
something they know,
when it's clear they don't know that much
and they've learnt it all from books.
The words they use aren't their own.

I found whole worlds of cerise and electric blue
and brought them into our house in little cupped hands, like
Here, look what I found for you.

I'd adamantly dance my head off
for any audience.
I was just copying me mum.

My parents were young enough,
and mad enough,
to know exactly what I was on about
when I talked complete shit
about the people in the woods
and the fairies up my nose,
about the bumdots and the pindits,
not humouring me, but joining in
with their own delicious twaddle.
They hadn't finished being kids themselves yet.
Cluelessly mismatching lifestyles and laughing
and laughing and laughing
at biscuits.

We could make a funfair on the landing
using a chair, a sock and some Play-doh.
Lick a slug for a laugh

and get a dad who's been at work all day
to do a forward roll
and mark him out of ten for it.

We didn't know what we were meant to be
so we just were.
We made an entire world out of nothing.

The world wasn't there
to tell us we were wrong.
We spelt it so wrong it was baeutiful.

He looks like a secret
someone forgot.
A fairy made of twigs,
dust and trainers.

Hasty limbs sewn on,
deep pockets and hands that flick
and squander.
Holds his head
like he doesn't know where it is.
Wears his heart on his face.

He wants love all wrong,
pretends it doesn't matter.

Scared of growing small.
Scared of disappearing.
Scared of not being looked for.

Smiles
and breaks your heart.

5pm dark and wet,
lampposts live forever.
Hailstones' favourite time of year.

The Arndale thrives and thinks
it'll always be this way.
Smiles benignly,
gets fatter,
glistens with pride.

Buses get narky,
cat-head each other.
Cars wear hats and hurry.
Bus stops gossip and jangle.

The Big Wheel puffs out his chest.
Selfridges has good posture.
Tramps know the score and like my hair.

Oxford Road is scared,
pretends to be drunker.
Wishes it was taller,
wants to go home.

Too-many-bags-in-one-hand is raging at
Too-many-people-to-buy-for.
Their daughter (5) fairy-twirls, gleeful,
wand aloft in the doorway to Primark.

Every Scart Lead I've Not Understood

I am every one of my brother's Star Wars figures
and the dances I choreographed for them.
I am every Cornerhouse staff I've fancied
and the lives I've imagined with them.

I am everything I've ever glued to my own face
and everything I've got my fingers stuck in.
I am every book I've not understood
and every diary I've wanted to look in.

I am every toilet I've ever been sick, had sex or cried in.
I'm every Tiffany Bling I've feared
and wanted to be friends with.
I am everything I have ever drawn on my own knees.

I'm every scart lead I've not understood,
every hoodie I've wanted to hug and shag the arse off.
Every object I've personified,
every institution I've vilified.

I am every form I've filled in
and every tablet I've took.
Every doctor who's got me wrong
and every madman who's got me right.

I am every little old lady
who knew the meaning of life
and played with it in her pocket.
I am every glitter-filled space rocket I've flown at 3am.

I'm every cup of tea I've loved
and every pen I've chewed to death.
I am every dyslexic I've met who can see the full-bodied,
technicoloured world between words.

I am not every pinstripe-brained teacher
who is colour-blind to the world.

I am every chicken wire sculptor
who is forced to work in Kwik Save.
I am every emo kid with his heart in his head.
I am every teddy I've loved and tortured.

I am every wise woman to be taken for a fool.

Rain steals Sunshine's bag,
dangles it out the window,
pulls out her hairband,
holds it tight in his fist.
Sunshine sulks, pouts, frowns;
Rain is besotted,
tingles when she touches his belongings.

Hailstones bunked off today and sat in a field
wishing it was dark,
digs his nails into his palm
and holds his breath.

Wind is barely noticed,
sits at the front with her bag in her lap.
She loves her long tatty hair
and how it smells.

Hailstones' sister ran away.
She should be seventeen now.

Wind wafts her head from side to side,
sometimes closes her eyes,
has no friends in real life.

Hailstones' dad is Thunder.
Hailstones won't remember his twenties.

Rain will have a growth spurt.
Sunshine will notice, take control,
smile sweetly, fall in love.
Rain is good at sports.

Wind won't pass any exams.
Looks after her gran.
Never knew her mum.

"No good," gran says.

Sunshine and Rain will get married.
On that day they'll rainbow.

Wind likes the idea of auras,
keeps it from her gran.

Sunshine will expect the world.
Rain will work hard.

Hailstones will rage.

Wind will wait a while
before she tells the authorities
when her gran dies.

Hailstones will lie in the dark,
gnarled-up and threadbare.

Sunshine will become wrinkled,
cloudy and angry.
Rain will turn into drizzle.

Hailstones will reach a crossroads,
wander knowing nothing,
discover Buddhism and valium,
become Snow.

Wind will get a dog and call it Violet.

Hailstones will never have a big house
or know how much he inspires
the kids he works with.

Wind will go to day centres,
fall in love with women,
howl and turn circles.

Bumblebee Girl

She hides from her thirties in the spare room,
all screwball scramble on the broken bookshelf.
Crouches in the craft box with the fuzzy felts,
drinking tea through a curly straw.

Etch A Sketches a new life:
spilled glitter in the playground.

She doesn't think in words
all one at a time,
thinks in sugar, pastels, bits of paper, Fraggles.
Loves the splosh of rain and Culture Club.

Last night she did the dishes with no top on
and sunglasses, lights alive and rainbow bright,
then punished the Cocoa Pops
in the twirly lid of the big yellow teapot.

She paints giant starships,
covers every inch,
works fast and lonely,
feasts on dried lavender and butterscotch.
Tiny silver stars
get caught in her throat.

Tiny dot trannies and tiny dot nuns.
Tiny dots in the bath having tiny dot fun.

Tiny dots jealous of their tiny dot peers.
Tiny dots with sticky out tiny dot ears.

Tiny dots shopping and tiny dots prayers.
Tiny dots unsure why they're having affairs.

Tiny dots getting lost trying to change at train stations.
Tiny dots in the dark having big revelations.

Tiny dots wearing the same sannie pad for three days.
Tiny dots up all night writing tiny dot essays.

Tiny dots wishing they'd never had kids.
Tiny dots planning their takeover bids.

Tiny dots getting pissed off and stealing tiny dot cars.
Tiny dots being thrown out of tiny dot bars.

Tiny dots singing, tiny dots waging wars.
Tiny dots scared of opening tiny dot doors.

Tiny dots setting off tiny dot smoke alarms.
Tiny dots cutting their tiny dot arms.

Tiny dots enjoying tiny dot anal sex.
Tiny dots looking for tiny dot specs.

Tiny dots without answers, tiny dots without friends.
Tiny dots saying sorry and making amends.

Tiny dots saying their final goodbye.
Tiny dots sighing a tiny dot sigh.

Tiny dots unravelling and becoming undone.
Tiny dots thinking they're the only one.

Chapter 2
The Moon

"They are slow-plod pleased with the pace
of sitting still and smiling in their bellies."

On the Moon they eat hefty vegetable stew
with thick-cut toast and butter
until tummy-chub happy
and big blanket heavy.

On the Moon they drink full-fat hot chocolate
from chunky mugs,
wrapped up in furry cardies,
lounging on big hairy rugs
made from dressing gown fluff.

They are slow-plod pleased with the pace
of sitting still and smiling in their bellies.

On the Moon they don't say *I love you*.
They just know.

Remember a Feeling

Remember this feeling.

When your belly's full
and good and grateful
the room glows orange and fat and smiles.
Happy thoughts laze about, content,
all warm and snug in your heavy head
and nothing needs to ever change.

Remember this feeling.

Head high, arms swinging,
wild flowers, tree tops and ready.
Something like God without the theories,
something like God with a twinkle in his eye,
and the river is delighted for you.
Wiggle your toes and laugh at the beauty and absurdity.
The world can be whatever it wants.

Remember this feeling.

On the edge of the sea
and aware of the depth and the distance,
miles from anyone, immersed in thisness
where meaning hangs heavy;
remembering to breathe as the flies slowly leave,
the clouds clear and the sea parts,
and words emerge and etch a path.

Every day Bumblebee Girl walked the mile into town to Dixon's to buy After Eight mints.

Every day she came home with nothing, more disheartened and pissed off than the day before.

After twenty-five years, one of the cashiers slipped a note into her pocket. It read:

We don't sell after 8 mints, we're an electrical shop, try a sweet shop, or Quality Save next to the bus stop.

So she did.

Rocket Boy 2

Stares me square in the shoulder,
unblinkingly alert,
zooming
in every direction at once.

Exploring the cosmos
and getting it *completely*,

and mouthing the meaning to life
in an impossible language
made of shapes,
and sparkling right here

like a rocketship made of tinfoil and paint,
flying and knowing
exactly what the Moon is
trying to say.

is the magical economy
of council house mothers
who conjure up food from nothing
and can't add up.

She's five foot four and taller than you.
Mascara, black hair, and lipstick-red polemics,
a Scouse Snow White.
Runs on tea-fuelled willpower,
love and gumption.

She curls her hair, does the splits and goes to Asda
(ooh la la!).
Can drive without the know-how,
drive without a license
to save her kids' lives.
Could drive without a car if she had to.

She invented Father Christmas
in a community centre in Ashurst.
She invented keep fit and leg warmers,
magicked up a dance school in the palm of her hand
from neon, stencils and guts.
Cooked up cerise and electric blue with no oven.

She knows what Robbie Williams is choking on
when he tries to talk to the Moon.
Stalked by The Beatles,
channels Nancy Sinatra,
and dances it better.

Everything she walks on is a dance floor.

She shimmies shammy leathers and Fab Cafés,
Ocky Tocky Ungers and calligraphies round her handbag,
discovered The Cavern and
made a made-up town from Sticklebricks
when she was just seventeen.
Made poetry from Alphabites,
kept Rainbow Brite bright

and made a town when she seventeen.

She lives
on Weetabix,
slidey floors,
and has the poshest of doors on every room.
Does her back in and keeps on trampolining.
Queen of coats,
cushions, charity shops and caring.
Would never let your feet go cold
or show an inch of disapproval.

Knows the importance of imaginary donkeys
and tiny doors in trees.

In the Connie
hard-arsed scallies
remember green cats,
ginn sheets and acceptance.
Hug her,
love her,
and call her Mrs Hagan.

Broughton

(There's a Netto near mine where,
if you don't concentrate,
a rocketship will come and fly you away.

There's a bus stop near mine where,
if you stand still too long,
a rocketship will come and take you to space,

full throttle sparkle up in the air,
weightless and real
life: a spot in the distance.

See, in Broughton, we fly rocketships.)

One day Bumblebee Girl was sitting in the dark. She imagined she could see lots of things.

She saw the outline of a witch, one of those children who age too quickly smirking at her, an unformed Siamese Twin and a noose dangling from the lampshade.

She started to freak out a bit, and tried to imagine she could see a unicorn glinting with stardust, a glitter-filled ice cream sundae and lots of friendly fairies smiling benignly.

Eventually she turned on the light and all of the things were there.

Chapter 3
The Bus Stop

"An empty Tropicana takes roll call . . ."

Free newspaper carpet underfoot,
bags are moved with martyrdom,
the in-lane knees poke out self-righteously,
the fat feel insecure.
Bags at the front are worried for at the back
and the smell of cannabis that's pumped on to buses
these days thrives.
An empty Tropicana takes roll call.

Top deck front left
giggles and squiggles in pigtails with mother,
crinkled bags of treasure: Primark, Etam,
disco wear for the under tens.
A sun-sheared arm shields
pink and glittered shrieks from

picky-kneed schoolgirl number one,
squeaks a carefully pilfered magic marker
Sophie loves Keven forever
I.D.S.T.
elbows generic schoolgirl number two,
a lacquered head with a hard girl fringe,
rampantly thinking of hopscotch on the rocks
and a way out.

Top deck front left nods a tinny heartbeat wound
on umbilical string,
stores a song to tune out every moment of life,
enjoys the onslaught of near misses with the trees
in Whalley Range,
keeps safely faceless face ahead.

A physics student in-jokes loudly down the phone
and no-one feels left out.

Topshop suit and tie
thinks he's undervalued,
watches every whispered twitch of

a freckle of a girl,
starched, pleated,
thinks in jitters, dotes for life,
grips an untattered file like an over-educated hamster,
falls in love for the second time today
with the faceless head in front:

flopsy hair, blazer, book,
sensitive outsider plimsolls,
keeps one on

bottom deck, disabled seat,
resident pissed git,
vacillating cock-eyed grin,
staggers whilst sitting for prey.

A lad in a tracksuit makes the best of an unfortunate haircut,
surreptitiously picks his nose, noticed by

bipolar shopping trip (regretting it already).

Pigtails and combats worries about nothing,
will cry about it later,
contemplates the suicide she'll never commit,
tries not to compare herself to

bottom deck, raised platform,
skin-tight thighs,
summertime cleavage at eye-level,
dashing in velour,
head to toe in Hollyoak pink,
bejewelled and bulbous,
discusses Shaun in the year above,
flaps her eyes at

bottom deck, heading to broken seat,
leg to the radiator,
sees it isn't raining but it could and always does,
sups on half a cup of foam to give him pep,
daydreams his life was worse.

A seen-the-world smile fakes back at
a boy with apologetic eyebrows and a grazed knee.

A man with a long neck leans forward and whispers something.

An empty Tropicana is tripped up by a corner,
rolls forward toward bottom deck driver's seat,
turns left, and jumps.

Veronica Pop

She hates WAGs, fags and carrier bags,
so up to date she can't remember yesterday.
Proving her popularity, her words lick your armpits.
Middle class, semi-detached and self-aware
in something stripy.
Has long pointless arms, is yet to pull a pint
and wears too little in the rain.

She thinks that cabaret is work-a-day,
believes she's in recovery,
gets nostalgic over Wac-a-Day,
does everything five times a day
and for Christmas wants robots and Reiki.
     Misuses the word *pikey*.

Collects puppets she never speaks to,
hand-knitted by someone else.
Does the Monster Mash on Thursdays,
the Time Warp on Fridays,
reflects the light on Saturdays
and by Sunday is cold, white and ironic.
     Prefers Mario to Sonic.

She's shiny and tiny, slip on, slip off;
thinks up well meant graffiti on nights off.
Still too inhibited to put pen to wall.

Wishes she was still in school,
sick of choosing the latest look.
Still can't say the word *fuck*
without looking over her shoulder.
Wants to smoulder, doesn't know how.
Wants to look up.

She's post-post-modern
and fits in your pocket,
like a keyring with nothing on it.

A grudging slave to positivity.
Acute, sincerely stuck,
he talks at right angles.

Opinions carefully chosen like a seating plan.

Consistently consistent,
like a suit
on a man
who always wears a suit.

A sci-fi figure kept in the box,
struggling to stay in it.

Bursts into the room
all arms and ideas.

Frantic shyness,
his fringe can't cope,
his mouth explodes,
can't shut up,
eyes like lasers.
A quickfire round.

Gobbledygook and wisdom
mesmerising like a bank robbery.
Beguiling,
like pornography.

Lindy Hop

She's merry-go-rounds at the seaside,
the pitter of rain on rooftops,
the patter of chaos; she's hopscotch,
cashmere pop socks.

She's the girl you met on holiday when you were thirteen.
You remember her hair
and how you wished you'd touched it.
Her name might be a lie you told yourself.

Pillows,
soft cotton summers,
believes in fairies just enough to get by.

She's smooth, confusing and soothing,
like childhood,

tells storybook lies.

The same girl
in knee socks,
kicks off
at 4am
with a very tatty head.

Keep Talking Chris   For Chris Murray

Keep talking Chris,
like a spirograph,
bounce back and forth like maths wrapped up in flowers,
spiralling like dancing with never ending stories.
Intricate, like snowflakes.
Simple and psychedelic,
like laughter.

So, stay
and tell me
about Ireland,
Theresa,
and being inside,

how long you haven't drank for,
the bands I need to hear
and the beauty in Tango cans.

You hand around compliments
like Fisherman's Friends,
your flattery makes no sense.
Like God doesn't.

You makes things happen and fizz in my head, Chris,
with the strength of a thousand unknown soldiers
and hindsight the history books can't stomach.
Gentle as Palma Violets.
Real as memory.

Your smile makes me know I know things
and you know things.
God, you can tell you were young once!
The world doesn't know what to do
with people like you.

Stubbornly cerise like light in your eyes.
Flashes her teeth: stardust, coiffured.

Makes you feel short,
like a jacket potato.

My Wednesdays are sat scrunch-backed
on the bus
at 8am.
Squeezed in,
smelling each other's sweat,
scared their lives are somewhere else
living themselves while they look the other way.
My Wednesdays believe crumple-hearted
in true and false and tying your hair back.
Sans serif,
A4,
and neatly placed back in the box.

Wednesday: like a broken paperclip.
Wednesday: like dry toast.
Wednesday: like a bit of a cold.
At very best, the Betterware catalogue.
The traffic jam of the week.

I want my Wednesdays to bloom!

Be ripe and full of fruit;
be real days,
tasty days,
juicy vibrant laughing days,
days as big as fields.

I want these stale,
small
Wednesdays
to edge into evening,
cool and fresh,

get home and take off their clothes,
breathe in

and
out,
full-lunged,

follow their *own* desire lines,
walk the whole way
swinging their arms and singing
at the top
of their tiny scared voices.

Chapter 4
The Waiting Room

"It's all in your head . . ."

One day Bumblebee Girl looked up and saw a tiny red dot, high up in the distance, very very far away.

She squinted and saw that it was a big red double-decker bus.

She tried to run away, but every time she looked up the big red bus was there, heading straight for her head.

She lived for many years with the knowledge of the big red bus. Sometimes she looked up, mainly she didn't.

One day it hit her.

Eric paces out the past
with fists as big as tower blocks.

Cat Diazepam daydreams softly:
poking her toe in a warm cup of tea,
eating jelly cubes,
having her hair brushed;
the hot squishy guilt.
Cat Diazepam smiles odd,
likes bobbles, gin and jam.
Got stuck early,
walks too slowly
and eats with her mouth open.
Has a large bottom she knows nothing of,
can't pronounce certificate.
Doesn't need to.

Nearly Graham stares at Jenga.

Bobby Bookshop smokes his own fingers.
Keeps it tight and smiley,
keeps his bad knees to himself.
Doesn't know where to go
and goes there,
gleeful,
mindless,
spins on the spot.
Paints lopsided smiles on jumble sale dolls,
whispers the lines to foggy-brained puppets.

Nearly Graham stares at Jenga.

Florence Nonsense bouffants,
embarrassed she isn't here.
Shouldn't.

Teeters, stretched
at the thought of visitors
and dirty cups.
Florence Nonsense thinks love
is a rumour.
Can't remember school
but thinks she didn't like it.
Uses fairy liquid as shampoo,
thinks she's the only one.
Feels something and drinks.
She's the only one.

Nearly Graham stares at Jenga.

Rocket Boy and the Felt-Tip Pens

"He's all head that lad,"
his mum used to say.
Dad spoke to other dads
in the family:
   "He's not interested in football."

He'd sit at home on sunny days,
not interested in football, entranced
by the closed curtained kingdom of Kunga-Foona Plate,
the secret world of Rabbit Calling
and the order of the colour of felt-tip pens.

From light to dark through the toned phases of
happy and sad, the families that didn't speak,
the lonely beige, bloody silly pink,
the disillusioned skin-tight grey.

Smarties got the treatment, too.
Lilac with a heart of gold and bubbles in its mouth
paired up with brown with curled up fists,
jealous yellow's forced to live with orange.

Sticklebricks sometimes matched Quality Street:
the long thin yellow
like Tuesdays and 7,
taller than him and just beyond reach;
and knew less in a different way.

The square in the circle of the blue one
made him itch,
but the planets made sense:
big Jupiter with over-succulent lips,
puffy, and he,
little Mercury,
not interested in football.

Neptune lived in the woods
with beautiful hair,
flourished with Pluto.

Mars was the bit of him
that kicked off,
teared and red,
knew every dinosaur by name
and faced the wall to sleep.

1
2
3
4 was ok,
corners and safe,

   "It's all in your head,"
they say to him now,
but it took three hours yesterday.

The Angry Crocodile

When he was six the Angry Crocodile kicked off in the playground. He threw his lunchbox at the railings and screeched and got his name.

When he went to high school, teachers looked at him, scared, expectant. The Angry Crocodile kicked off to fill a hole.

The people in the Angry Crocodile's town would cross the road and swerve their eyes when they came near him. The Angry Crocodile kicked off to make them see.

The Angry Crocodile's family got used to him kicking off. The Angry Crocodile kicked off to fulfil a role.

When he was old enough the Angry Crocodile started going to a pub called *The Angry Crocodile* because he was lonely. The Angry Crocodile kicked off because he didn't know what to say.

When he was in his thirties the Angry Crocodile got a girlfriend who renamed him Bob.

Cat Diazepam's Morning Face

You can't escape her morning face,
it hangs awkwardly off her head,
threatening to flop forward
Splash!
into her tea.

It slumps, featureless,
like a damp futon mattress;

heavy and unhappy,
like a passive aggressive cupboard.

It squints at the world,
expecting the worst.
Narkily can't comprehend
anything more complex than
a cup.

Takes a long grumpy time
to sit up straight
and look the world
in the world's
morning face.

"The electronic mouse deterrent I got to deter the mouse
deters me more than the mouse.
It spikes into the room,
huge,
every couple of seconds.

"In the same way fan heaters and hairdryers shoot
long tightly permed zig-zags into the air
that slowly straighten out
the further away you get.

"TV scramble makes
a million tiny pockets of air
empty that vibrate,
panic,
and demand attention.

"Crisp packets shoot needles
and glass without looking
where they're going.

"The traffic outside creates a big soft flow of flatness.

"The computer buzz is infinitely
tiny
shaky
dots
that sometimes shoot around the screen in packs.

"Deep bassy voices smack
big flat steel walls
forward and backwards,
again
and again."

Children are not small adults.

A is for Airway.
If you lay a young child flat,
her big head can cause serious airway problems
by forcing the chin onto the chest
in an exaggerated position.
I had eight imaginary friends, now I have none.

B is for Burns.
I cut my hand open when I was twenty-one
separating two frozen pies with a bread knife.

C is for Cervical Spine and Car Seats.
Boy George was my hero:
"Everyone has a broken neck until proven differently."

D is for Drowning.
Toddlers are perpetually curious creatures.
Bucket drownings occur as children find a bucket,
look curiously inside, and then fall in because of the
way their big heads affect their centre of gravity.

E is for Environment (and Everything Else).
Children should be kept pink, warm and sweet.
When I was twelve
I stabbed my friend in the knee
with safety scissors.

When I was twenty-three
I did it again.

My Dad

On Father's Day the cemetery's full
and I want to make some friends
with angry daughters
who are still rebelling
against the biggest deadline they ever missed.

I want to tell them things
and run away,
hope they hadn't listened.

I want to walk around with flowers
and pretend I'm good at grief.

But I'm in someone else's cemetery.
I've never been to the right one.

So I pretend it's cos I don't buy into heaven
and it's cos I do things differently.

But there are some things I don't do at all.

You need to paint a landscape,
you need to make it good,
your life depends on it,
but all you have is half a potato and a splodge of blue paint.

Come on!
Hurry up!
Quick!

(Or we won't help you.)

When it's like untangling the biggest box of coat hangers
and you have to start somewhere,
it's never *Once upon a time . . .*

But I see what you mean
when words are stitched together with broken wool
and the breaths between tell the real story.

When what you mean is curled up so small,
like a pea under a hundred mattresses.

When the words are all lies,
a million miles from a story you need to tell and hide.
Gagging on shame,
throat packed in with blame and desperate,
right down to the fingertips, to change.
Victims aren't saints.

When words are the last thing on your mind
and you need to talk.
You need to talk,
but not about this,
about anything but this.

When optimism tastes like plastic

and your smile is made of concrete,
and you can't be force-fed any more positivity.

When you're wide awake and stoic,
but the future is too far away
and breath won't come.

When every little hair
is alert to every imagined danger.

When the front door looms.
When there's too many objects.
When you can't take another face.
When you can't handle the order of the alphabet.

The words you use don't matter
and what I say won't solve it,
but maybe it helps
that I really do know what you mean.

Chapter 5
The Bedroom

"Sex that's grubby, sparkling and honest."

Tea and Coffee

When I was born they said:
    "I bet she'll like coffee."
The right chromosomes you see,
and I cared not a jot,
happy with my breast milk.
I didn't understand why everyone
was so het up about hot drinks.

But time passes and I turned twelve,
started to look at mugs, china cups;
saw the tea my father chain-drank,
the coffee my mother savoured.
Figured either would do to douse my thirst.

Looked up with childish glee and saw tall faces:
    "You will drink coffee,
    you will admire coffee,
    you will fall in love with coffee,
    settle down with coffee,
    you will serve coffee all your goddamn life."

Didn't think it was worth asking about tea.

So I did drink coffee.
I drank it by the gallon:
tried instant coffee against the back walls of clubs;
tried espresso, found it was over too soon;
tried filter coffee, who told me to lose weight;
tried latte which was just
too phlegmy.

Coffee was jittery,
didn't know where to put its hands,
thought it was something special if I at least enjoyed it.
Coffee was demanding:
I must wear make up and a dress;

requested I pluck my eyebrows,
moaned about my breasts.
Coffee wanted me to wank it off in the middle of the night.

Eventually I asked:
   "It's alright this coffee, but have you got anything else?"
   "Oh yes my dear, but it's not for you!
   You like coffee, remember?
   Coffee fulfils you completely."
   "Oh."
Kinder ones replied:
   "Maybe you just haven't had the right cup of coffee yet."

But coffee was fine, it did the job,
it was hot and wet
and I wasn't thirsty afterwards.

But that I'm told we mustn't do
becomes just that which we pursue
and I was surrounded
without censor
by sexy, curvy, sweet cups of tea,
slurped carelessly by boys and men.
   "It's not for you!"
   "But my father loved tea!"

I flirted relentlessly but knew I couldn't drink it.
(Didn't know why I couldn't drink it.)
Thought I'd really like to try it.
(Felt ashamed I'd like to try it.)
. . . Couldn't help but try to try it.

So, under the pretence of seeking a university degree
came to Manchester, in ravenous search for tea.

And tea leaks out Manchester's walls!
University life is filled with tea:
crusty, dreadlocked, herbal tea;
daddy, Prada, Earl Grey tea;

enthusiastic new found tea with asymmetric hair-dos.

There's tea meetings, shops and clubs.
There's even a tea drinkers' pub!

And tea took me, nourished me, let me be me,
in pyjamas, unshaven, unplucked.

Tea fucked me like tea does.

Didn't shriek at menstruation
or react with indignation when I wouldn't wank it off.
Didn't moan about my breasts, for tea had breasts too!
Went on a bit about goddesses
but tea knew where to put its hands
and I knew how to treat tea.

And what a surprise: tea was better at it then me!

But the world of tea it seems, is not itself without restriction,
for tea drinkers can't help but force the conviction
I must drink only tea,
when they found out I'd slurped
a cup of coffee that very morning.

They said coffee was against us,
said that coffee was the enemy,
all caffeine is rape,
and, with a exhausted sense of déjà vu,
I grew sick of this dichotomy of
just what it is I must not do.

And remember, that we must not do,
becomes just that which we pursue
and coffee leaks out Manchester's walls!

I learnt to avoid the phlegmy coffee,
the coffee that just wanted to watch me drink tea.
Found coffee that knew where to put its hands,

and coffee took me, nourished me, let me be me,
in pyjamas, unshaven, unplucked.

Coffee fucked me like coffee does.

But like The Beatles and The Rolling Stones
I mustn't admit to enjoying both,
and in a quandary lived a double life . . .
and slowly noticed the world was rife with those who
want their coffee *and* their tea;
drink one in public, the other secretively.
(The same who bawl with self-righteous anger
that I must choose.)

Weary of hypocrites,
for they protest too much,
I held up my head
and took a mug,
a tea bag,
and a spoonful of coffee,
and stirred
and stirred.
And didn't stop when they objected,
didn't stop when they rejected me
from tea drinking clubs.

And now, when I drink tea
they call me a tea drinker;
when I sup coffee,
a coffee drinker.

But they know I do both.

I drink tea,
I drink coffee.
Because they both whet my whistle.

Sex Like Sex

There's a kind of sex where I don't feel a thing.
Sex like nodding and smiling
when you're not really listening.
Sex like murmuring the answer
so they don't know you're wrong,
when you think you might be right,
but you might be wrong.
Sex like collecting empty vodka bottles.
Sex like texting.
Sex like crisps.
Sex like smalltalk.
Sex like sex like sex like . . .
where you don't really touch each other.

I want sex where I'm there.
Sex like delighted oversharing,
like telling me the in-between bits of your childhood
where words don't fit together
and you have to use your hands instead,
like telling me the things that don't make sense,
that scare you, that scare me, too.
Sex like looking up beyond the treetops and
pressing my hands into the mud.
Sex like confident shoplifting.
Sex like summing up in full-bodied words
what you've been trying to say for ages.
Sex like someone really listening.
Sex that's grubby, sparkling and honest.
Sex like sex like sex like . . .
where you really touch each other.

A gleaming sliver,

gasping dreams,
timid
with sky-high quivering hope.

Life
breathed into
a choked-up chance to be real.

Real as daytime and sweet black coffee.
Real as everything you've ever wanted.

So, on tippy-toes, you hold your breath.

    Crick . . . crick . . . crick
      (a rollercoaster)
                Crick . . . crick . . . crick
                  (and higher
till your breath can see the sea.)

There.
      Stop.
That moment.
      Stop.
Before
             whoooosh . . . . . !
                        plunged and sudden running too
fast with light in your eyes holding your breath screaming laughter
like sneezing six times in a row letting go full throttle talking ten to
the dozen like sneezing six times in a row a thousand people cycling
in traffic the dreams are made . . .
                  . . . made real to the touch.

Tea, laughter and light.

Tea, laughter and light and
vast, fresh, green, real
as the taste of
scratched cotton grass.

Whirlwinded still.

Cup of tea content at the sky.

Midday warm.

Breathing new air.

Pre-loved is a Popple,
nostalgic, unfashionable and short.
The back of her hand is light blue beige
from thirty years of notes to self.

On her knee, a small groove the size of a lovers' tiff.
An ear sucked clean off with love,
a threadbare bum; knows the score,
doesn't really pluck or fake it anymore.

One eye is held on by a thread.
They say they'll sort it in June,
but pre-loved Popple can wait.

Lopsided scars,
little staggering hatred,
curious oddball fears.
It's the dents that make you interesting.

Perfect silver sphere.
I prefer jumble sales,
the horsefly of the eccentric.
The smell of soil sewn in the scrap.

A chewed-off ear of a Transformer,
the chewed-off skin around your nails,
the chip in the mug.
The wonky story bits.

The broken bits fixed,
the broken bits broken.
The dark corners and under the table.

The loved so hard it hurts,
the loved too little.
The little that tells a story.

Rocket Boy and Bumblebee Girl

He holds his hands behind his back
and says,
"Choose one."
She smiles, says "Left."

Rocket Boy likes straight lines and goals.
Bumblebee Girl like veils, light and water.

He holds her hand and squeezes,
is good at saying things,
good strong things set in stone.
Things that last forever.

She shifts, itchy in her seat,
feels every millimetre of change,
vibes smack her in the face.
Feels the breath of a man behind her,
can sense the lies he told this morning.
Can feel a TV on stand-by from a hundred metres.
Knows what knickers you wear, the age you'll thrive,
what siblings you should've had, what's on your back.

Rocket Boy knows these things are real.
At first he thought she was psychic.

Bumblebee Girl walks a different way home every night.
Rocket Boy gets the bus.

He holds his hands behind his back
and says,
"Choose one."
She smiles, says "Left."
He smiles and gives her both.

Deep Down Happy   For Brink

A thick deep forest,
the kind of midnight that crunches underfoot,
a tiny blue door in the trunk of a tree
the size of fairies (the kind of thing not everyone can see).

Inside she was crouched,
tail wrapped, talons dug deep,
waiting to be freed.
Nails bitten, horns hidden,
jeans ripped, wings curled,
knees to her chest,
tear-stained, couldn't breath.

And someone took her hand.

She unfurled.
Untangled her wings.

Stretched out magic top to toe,
took a full breath from the sky,
looked you right in the eye
and smiled
a million year smile.
And renamed herself
Deep Down Happy.

Deep Down Happy is earth blood-thick chunky wood
nourished right to her fingertips,
belly-good grateful right to her toes.
Takes full bites.
Life size.

Deep Down Happy has special powers:
can unpick knots and give directions.
Is immortal.

☺ Not really.
But knows the secret
in the sigh of the bus when it leaves, and . . .

the importance of tiny doors in trees.

She's tea and the Moon and everything in-between.
She really feels.

She bakes,
makes cakes.
Makes sense without trying to.

Muscles relaxed,
she's soft, warm,
candle wax.

Can stay still.

Fully rounded and grounded like tree trunks in snow,
she *is* snow, thick deep snow.
The kind that sticks around for years.

Deep Down Happy 2

Deep Down Happy eats quiche with her saviour and feels
the childhood feeling of belonging
before you knew it could get lost.

He never hurts her brain
with too much sense at once.
Can make 2 + 2 be 4, and just as equally 5,
73,
or Carebear.

Can talk straight lines with businessmen
whilst winking nonsense at her and crafting a story for later.
Scales scaffolding at midnight doused in magic and cider,
charms clouds into thunderstorms to sing her to sleep.

His inside coat
pockets singing mice,
rats in tops hats, a dandy hamster.
Jangles with broken pocket watches
that tell every time.

He keeps four self-propelled teddy bears with tails,
the chosen ones; fluffy with pride,
they wink back at him.

He is there for her in sleep
and on waking tells her how right she is to be.
Hops dreams like stepping stones,
brings frogs out of themselves
and brought Bambi's mum back to life.

She lays gentle-bathed and rain-patted.
The edges of her happy ending novel
poke the suds.

We don't see in black and white,
we dream in technicoloured cabarets
of multicoloured shopping trolleys.

We know how savage hope is,
the incongruity of some chairs
and the magic mothers weave.

Need to leave the 9-to-5 for those it's for
and dress to the hilt
in beauty, disgust and cosmic dust.

We know that cup's wearing lippy
cos it's getting ready for a night on the town
with Pat, its best mate, who's a whisky drinking saucer.

We know how funny peas are (and that they're Geordies),
that curtains are eyelids,
and that people are people no matter what they're doing.

We know that apostrophes mean
fuck all.
We're easily enthralled and appalled,
know there's a thousand billion sides to every story,
to every word,
to every intake of breath;
know the reality and unreality of death.

We know how multicoloured blue is,
how full-bodied grey is,
and the very differing personalities
of the letters of the alphabet.
We don't so much question,
as know this answer's one of many.

We know that words are just building blocks,
simple-minded shapes in primary school colours: toys.

That language is a framework,
like holding water together.

We've always existed.
In our time been burned as witches,
called empaths, shamans, gurus,
stupid flighty bitches,
deranged, frivolous or, hilariously, oblivious,
pernickety, irrational, over-sensitive, ridiculous,
dyslexic, perplexing, too intense and always wrong,
and made to feel like we never belong.

Been exploited, beaten, and electroshocked,
been kept in the attic, been mocked, forgotten,
had our powers twisted by insistent psychiatrists,
or stolen by tablets and tablets and tablets and tablets . . .

Been patronised to shit, dismissed as fools,
and had our wings shorn early by the hell of school.

Bent and twisted out of shape,
we've flown inward and wilted,
or soared.
And if none of that,
ignored.

See how strong the world tastes in our mouths?
It's no wonder we really do talk to the Moon

Acknowledgements

Thank you to the following people / organisations / animals / bands / imaginary friends for the support / inspiration / friendship / pints / gigs / funding / laughs / love: Brink, Mum, Our Mike, conor a, Ange Middleton, Steve Lyons, Gerry Potter, Vanessa Fay, Net Raw, Michelle Green, Joyce Pratt, Clare Garner, Fergus Evans, Rachel van der Bergen, Dominic Berry, Rod Tame, Steve O'Connor, Chris Dommett, Dermot Glennon, Amanda Milligan, Trish Ashworth, John Leyland, Melanie Rees, Rachael K, Lisa B, Rosie Garland, Mike Wilson, Vivien Peach, Tony Walsh, Tony Curry, Dom Harbot, Diane Scanlon, Annette Cookson, Gary McMahon, Stevie Turner, Simon O'Brien, Libby Tempest, Simon Rennie, David Hoyle, Chris Meehan, Cathy Bryant, Allan Gray, Clare Shaw, Yvonne Sewell, Matt Panesh, Mike Garry, John G. Hall, Emma at the greenroom, Shoeless Carole, the really enthusiastic girl at Absolutely Free, Mark Simpson, Steph Pike, Steffeny McGiffen, Steve Banbury, Martin Stannage, Graham Smyth, Sophie Parkes, Helen Love, Susan Matthews, Slowpoke, Tongue, Kunga Foona Plate, Callisto, Tess, Lumpy, Xerka, Lucinda, Carol Batton, Mr Havers, everyone at Survivors Poetry, BlueSCI Seymour Poets, Moodswings Network, greenroom, Commonword, Per Verse, Freed-Up, Scratch Poets, Poetry Pillow, Animal Writes and The Ineffables. Apples & Snakes and Contact theatre. Everyone in the Manchester Poetry Scene and all the people who stand at my bus stop who have no idea I have plagiarised their personalities and put them in a book.

Previous versions of 'A Made-Up Town' and 'Keep Talking Chris' first appeared in *The Ugly Tree #20*, Feb '09 [ed. P. Neads, Flapjack Press], and 'Tea and Coffee' in *Shut Your Eyes and Put Out Your Hand* [Citizen32, 2007]. Credit and thanks to Apples & Snakes and Incubate for the use of 'The Wisdom of the Jumble Sale', 'The Moon is Fat', 'Zen', 'My Mum', 'Big Head Little Body Syndrome', 'Pre-Loved' and 'The Little That Tells a Story', earlier versions of which were written as part of *Belief-O-Matic* at Contact theatre in 2009.